HAYWARDS HEATH
TO SEAFORD

Vic Mitchell and Keith Smith

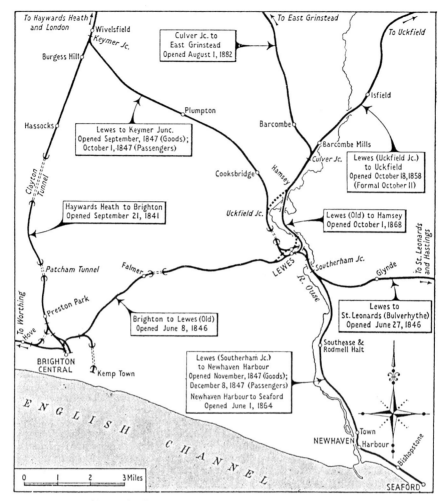

Chronological map of the railways around Lewes

(Railway Magazine)

Published March 1986
Reprinted November 2005

ISBN 0 906520 28 2

© *Middleton Press, 1986*

Design   Deborah Esher
Typesetting   Barbara Mitchell

Published by
         Middleton Press
         Easebourne Lane
         Midhurst, West Sussex
         GU29 9AZ
Tel: 01730 813169
Fax: 01730 812601
Email: info@middletonpress.co.uk
www.middletonpress.co.uk

Printed & bound by Biddles Ltd, King's Lynn

CONTENTS

ACKNOWLEDGEMENTS

We would like to thank those mentioned in the photograph credits for the assistance received and our gratitude goes to Mrs E. Fisk, N. Stanyon and our wives for help with the text. We are particularly glad to have R.C. Riley associated with this album. His factual and photographic contributions have been considerable; his local knowledge has helped immensely and his position as Historical Adviser to the Association of Railway Preservation Societies authenticates his work. Thanks are also due to N. Langridge for the loan of many of the tickets.

GEOGRAPHICAL SETTING

The Haywards Heath area is about 200ft. above sea level, being situated on the sandstones of the Hastings Beds. The line drops from there southwards onto the Wealden Clay and runs roughly parallel to the South Downs until reaching Lewes. This ancient town occupies a strategic position overlooking the gap in the Downs cut by the River Ouse and through which the railway passes with minimal engineering problems. The line runs close to the east bank of the river almost to its mouth at Newhaven where it turns east to hug the shoreline until reaching the Downs-foot town of Seaford.

The Ordnance Survey maps reproduced in this album are to the scale of 25" to 1 mile, unless otherwise stated.

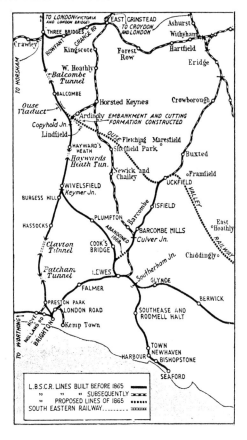

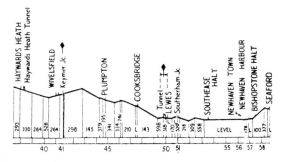

(Railway Magazine)

HISTORICAL BACKGROUND

The railway from London to Brighton was completed in 1841 and in 1846 a line was constructed across the Downs from Brighton to Lewes. The more direct link from Lewes to the main line at Keymer Junction was opened to passengers on 1st October 1847. From this line, a branch ran northwards to Uckfield from 1858 until 1868 when it was rebuilt on a more direct route into Lewes.

The Lewes to Newhaven section was opened for passenger traffic on 8th December 1847 and a single line extension to Seaford was brought into use on 1st June 1864. This was doubled in 1904 and singled again in 1975.

The Horsted Keynes branch through Ardingly was brought into use on 3rd September 1883, linking the main line to the East Grinstead to Lewes route, the latter having been opened in the previous year.

All the lines in the area were initially operated by the London Brighton and South Coast Railway and that company chose to develop Newhaven as their port for cross channel traffic.

History was made on 1st January 1933 when electric traction was introduced on the main line to Brighton, electrification of the route covered by this album taking place on 7th July 1935. The only section to have been closed is that between Horsted Keynes and Haywards Heath (on 28th October 1963), although the branch as far as Ardingly remains in use for the carriage of road stone.

RAILWAY SHIPPING SERVICES

Cross channel traffic commenced in a small way over 20 years before the railway reached Newhaven. By the 1860s, the LBSCR and the Chemin de Fer de l'Oeust were jointly in control of the passenger traffic and much of the goods traffic also. Around 40,000 passengers were carried annually.

From April 1889, sailings could be made regardless of the state of the tide and by 1893 a regular day and night service carried 111,600 passengers in the year. In 1903, the figure was 202,000 – success indeed.

The harbour was closed to commercial traffic on 12th August 1914 until 5th March 1919, passenger services being recommended in July.

Passenger figures fluctuated considerably between the Wars, reaching a peak of 383,000 in 1938. There was also a notable traffic in gold bullion – 173 tons per month in 1930, for example.

Service was again suspended in September 1939 but was resumed before the end of the war, on 19th January 1945. Fluctuating numbers brought about the withdrawal of winter passenger services from 1956 to 1964. In 1964 a revival began with the introduction of roll on/roll off facilities. A car sleeper train to Scotland was provided for a number of years in connection with this service.

In 1969, the name Sealink was introduced although the service was still operated by the French and British Railways until acquired by Sea Containers Ltd. in 1984.

BRIGHTON AND SOUTH COAST RAILWAY

NEWHAVEN & DIEPPE ROUTE   TO ALL PARTS OF THE CONTINENT

DECEMBER, 1922, or until further notice.

MARKET TICKETS
TO
LEWES
ARE ISSUED
Every SATURDAY

BY TRAINS LEAVING AT					FROM	RETURN FARES, Third Class.	
a.m.	p.m.	p.m.	p.m.	p.m.		s.	d.
10 9	—	1 54	4 32	6 9	SHEFFIELD PARK ...	**1**	**10**
10 15	—	2 3	4 38	6 18	NEWICK & CHAILEY	**1**	**7**
10 23	—	2 13	4 46	6 27	BARCOMBE		**10**
10 30	1 55	3 58	5 26	—	PLUMPTON	**1**	**1**
10 37	2 2	4 5	5 35	—	COOKSBRIDGE ...		**6**
10 43	—	2 47	5 18	6 44	ISFIELD...	**1**	**1**
10 49	—	2 54	5 25	6 50	BARCOMBE MILLS ...		**8**

Available to return by any Train day of issue only.

No luggage allowed. Children under three years of age, accompanying adult passengers, will be conveyed free. Children of three or more, but under twelve years of age, will be conveyed at half-fares.

The Railway Company give notice that tickets are issued subject to the conditions and regulations relating thereto and to the holders thereof set out in the Railway Company's Time Table Book. Passengers should ascertain if and where they must change carriages.

London Bridge Terminus,
November, 1922.

WILLIAM FORBES,
General Manager.

TRAIN SERVICES

When the Seaford branch opened there were six trains on weekdays and three on Sundays, 3rd Class passengers being allowed only on the first and last trains. 50 years later the service had increased to 11 trains, some of which ran to and from London.

The service was greatly augmented in 1906 with the introduction of railmotors. If available for service the two petrol railcars were used on some workings until their transfer to Departmental stock in 1911. The 1912 timetable shows 22 weekday trains between Lewes and Seaford, of which half were motor trains. On the Horsted Keynes branch there were ten trains, two of which terminated at Ardingly, while one worked to and from Oxted. The 7.43p.m. Brighton–London Bridge used this route. There were two motor train duties at Brighton shed affecting the Seaford branch. The first duty apart from branch trips made one trip each to Newick & Chailey, Three Bridges via East Grinstead, Uckfield and Haywards Heath. The only variant in the second duty was that it worked the 3.55p.m. Lewes–Sheffield Park, returning thence to Brighton. A similar pattern continued until electrification with minor variations.

With electrification, services were greatly increased and outside peak hours were on a regular interval basis, there being over 50 trains on the Seaford line, mostly the half hourly trains to and from Brighton but including two through trains to Victoria and one to London Bridge, as in the down direction. The morning peak train to London Bridge was combined with a train from Ore at Lewes, and they divided there in the evening peak, a practice which continues to this day.

The Horsted Keynes branch had 25 trains, mostly the hourly service to and from Haywards Heath. Inevitably the train service was reduced in WWII when the ample sidings at Horsted Keynes provided stabling for disused Pullman Cars. After the war the service to Seaford was much the same but with only an hourly service to and from Brighton, the intermediate trains coming from Lewes or in some cases Horsted Keynes, on which branch the service had been much reduced.

The Seaford services today consist of hourly trains to and from Brighton, augmented at peak hours, at which time the through service to and from London is retained.

A daily through train between Portsmouth Harbour and Newhaven Marine was tried in the summer of 1966.

In 1984 a through journey on Monday to Fridays to and from Hove (with Portsmouth connections) was introduced. In 1985, this was extended to start at Littlehampton at 05.13. A through service between Newhaven Marine and the North of England was announced in 1986, ironically the year in which the construction of the Channel Tunnel was also announced.

———————————————————

————————→

In 1892, a further Manning Wardle was purchased second-hand (makers no. 403 of 1872). It is seen in unlikely circumstances with the LBSCR armoured train used for manœuvres between 1894 and 1900. *Bradford* was sold to a Yorkshire contractor in 1898. Both engines were painted in LBSCR colours and if either were out of action, a Terrier was hired from that company. (National Army Museum)

NEWHAVEN HARBOUR COMPANY'S LOCOMOTIVES

Although to all intents and purposes Newhaven Harbour belonged to the LBSCR, early legislation required it to be controlled by an independent company. Initially it used horses to shunt its quayside lines but in 1881 bought this second-hand Manning Wardle, which was also used to haul loads of sand from the beach to Denton Cement Works. It was overhauled as needed at Brighton Works and scrapped in 1892. (SR Magazine).

Fenchurch was the first Terrier to be built and the first to be sold. She was purchased by the Harbour Co. in 1898 and is seen here in that company's livery. A brief history is given in our *Branch Line to Hayling* under her original number of 72. She is now a regular visitor to the first station in this album, being one of the Bluebell Railway's extensive locomotive fleet. (R.C. Riley collection)

HORSTED KEYNES

1. Our justification for extending this album to include Horsted Keynes is that an electric stopping train service operated between there and Seaford, prior to closure of the branch. The trains were then typically 2BIL units, as seen on the left of this April 1955 photograph. No. 42081, with one clean buffer, heads an Oxted to Brighton train and is about to leave for Lewes on what was to become the Bluebell line. The station is fully described and illustrated in our *Branch Lines to East Grinstead*. (S.C. Nash)

ARDINGLY

3. The 1883 buildings remained almost unchanged until closure. Only the roadside station house and offices survive today and can just be seen between the signal box and down platform canopy, in this turn of the century view. (Lens of Sutton)

1910 map

2. Before the Bluebell Railway was severed from BR a number of through excursions were worked. This is a return special to London Bridge on 1st April 1962, hauled from Sheffield Park by ex-LSWR 4–4–2T no. 488. The white boards by the leading wheels of the locomotive protect the northerly end of the branch conductor rail. (E. Wilmshurst)

SOUTHERN RAILWAY.
Issued subject to the Bye-laws, Regulations & Conditions in the Company's Bills and Notices.

Horsted Keynes to
Horsted Keynes   Horsted Keynes
Ardingly   Ardingly
ARDINGLY

THIRD CLASS   THIRD CLASS
Fare 6d   Fare 6d
NOT TRANSFERABLE.

9065

4. East of the station was the 218yd long Lywood tunnel and the Sheriffs Mill road bridge, a six arch viaduct. These structures deterred the Bluebell Railway from acquiring this branch but the tunnel was a blessing during a World War II air raid when a train that was being attacked by a German fighter plane took refuge in it. The driver of the 2BIL set has just given the token to the signalman. For the last few years of the line's existence, only the up line was in regular use. (J.H. Aston)

5. Graded roadstone from Somerset is discharged from hopper wagons in the building in the distance. The locomotive first runs round its train and propels half of it at a time for emptying. One of the two coating plants can be seen but the finely restored station building is to the left of the camera. It is used as offices by the Amey Roadstone Corporation. (H.C. Cooper/Bluebell Archives)

6. Apparently a train of infinite length. In reality it is a number of new 4CEP units stored on the down line prior to the introduction of electric services to the Kent coast. Twelve coach sets were taken in strict rotation on running-in trips to Polegate or Hastings. A motorman was employed all day on the branch, moving trains towards the junction so that those returning could join the back of the queue. After the first stage of the Kent Coast electrification in June 1959, the down line was used for the storage of condemned steam stock. (R.C. Riley)

7. A Centenary Special was operated on 3rd September 1983 and is seen passing the site of Copyhold Junction, which was only a true junction during the period that the branch was electrically operated. (P. Barnes)

London Brighton & South Coast Railway.

Ford Junction to

ARDINGLEY

HAYWARDS HEATH

910 map

Drill Hall

F.P.

Gas
Works

GREEN ROAD

P.O.

S.P.

S.P.

COMMERCIAL
SQUARE

S.P.

Timber Yd.

CATTLE
MARKET

Station
Hotel

MILTON ROAD

MARKET PLACE

Wharf

Station

Tk.

F.B.

STATION ROAD

Lodge

Bank

lice Station

rish Rm.

P.O.

Limehurst

Tk.

Cr.

S.M. W.M.
B.

Meth. Chap.
(Wes.)

YMOUNT ROAD

H E A T H

S.P.

ROAD

Council
Offices

8. Looking south in 1898, we see the two bay platforms and crossover provided at the north end of the station. On the left, a class D3 0–4–4T slumbers in a siding with some Stroudley stock. The timber platform extension is on the road bridge. This helps to locate the position today.
(O.J. Morris/Lens of Sutton)

9. At the south end of the station, a bay platform was provided on the down side only, adjacent to the goods shed. A roof partly covered its track, as at Three Bridges where the feature survived until more recent times.
(E.W. Jackson collection)

10. A D1 hauled push and pull set passes North Box on 19th July 1930. Both signal boxes were replaced by a new electric one on 12th June 1932. The bed-head style name-board, seen earlier, has been replaced with one of early SR design, manufactured at their Exmouth Junction concrete works. (H.C. Casserley)

London Brighton & South Coast Railway.

Newhaven Wh'f to
Shoreham

12. The changing style of Newhaven boat trains will become apparent in the course of this album. Here class 73 electro-diesel no. E6035 (later 73128) is about to enter the tunnel south of the station on 29th June 1969. (J. Scrace)

11. The buildings on the down side, together with the water tank (on the left) and the goods shed, werc demolished prior to electrification. The bays were abolished to make way for two 800ft island platforms. (Lens of Sutton)

13. The class 56 hauled empty stone train from Ardingly to Westbury makes an impressive sight as it leaves on 6th March 1985. The train is capable of carrying 1400 tons of stone and is so long that when it stops at Chichester station for crew changing, it obstructs the level crossing, bringing the city traffic to a standstill. (J. Scrace)

WIVELSFIELD

Wivelsfield Station, Sussex (showing the Through Manchester to Eastbourne Train coming from London).

14. The first station in this area was known as Keymer and was on the Lewes branch. It was opened on 1st January 1862 and was in use for exactly 21 years. The station on the main line, seen on this postcard, first saw passengers on 1st August 1886 but the train mentioned on it never stopped here. From 1905, it was known as the 'Sunny South Express'. (Lens of Sutton)

15. On 5th September 1983, we see the 14.53 Victoria - Eastbourne - Ore train, unusually composed of only one set, which was very crowded. By then, the station was one of the few on the main line to retain the characteristics of a rural LBSCR Victorian structure. (J.S. Petley)

KEYMER JUNCTION

16. We look south towards Brighton as a train from Eastbourne squeals on the check rails of the curve which has a 20mph speed restriction. The rear coach is by the foot-bridge seen in the next view, both pictures having been taken on 28th April 1971. (J. Scrace)

The 1875 edition shows the position of the first Keymer station which was in Cants Lane.

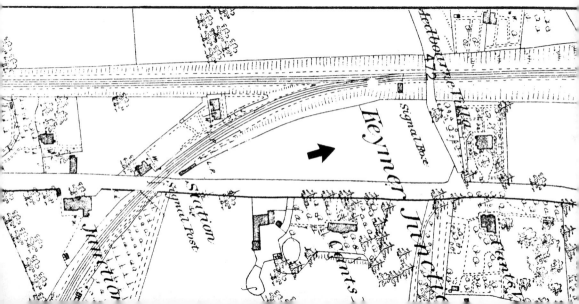

17. The junction signal box (and its privy) have now gone in favour of a more modern panel box at Three Birdges, which means fewer men (and toilets). The motorised junction points however have been prone to failure – John Keys, a leading railman at Wivelsfield, won an award in 1985 for keeping the trains running by winding the points by hand for over four hours. (J. Scrace)

London Brighton & South Coast Railway.

Ford Junction to

Horsted Keynes

Keymer Brick & Tile Works siding in 1897.

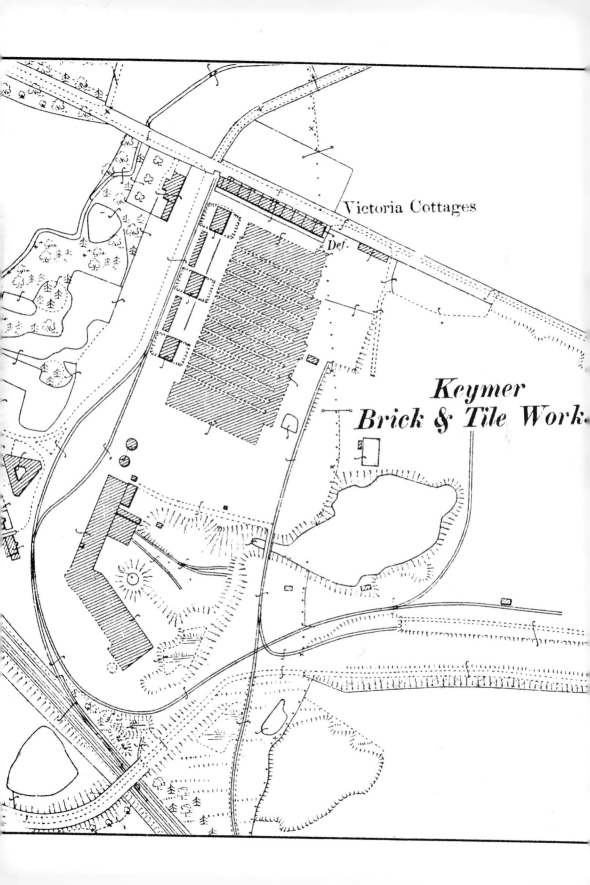

Victoria Cottages

Def.

Keymer
Brick & Tile Work

PLUMPTON

18. The village is nearly two miles to the south, at the foot of the Downs, but residential development occurred just north of the station, known as Plumpton Green. LBSCR features worth noting are the great length of the signal arm and the hollow warning disc on the gate. (Lens of Sutton)

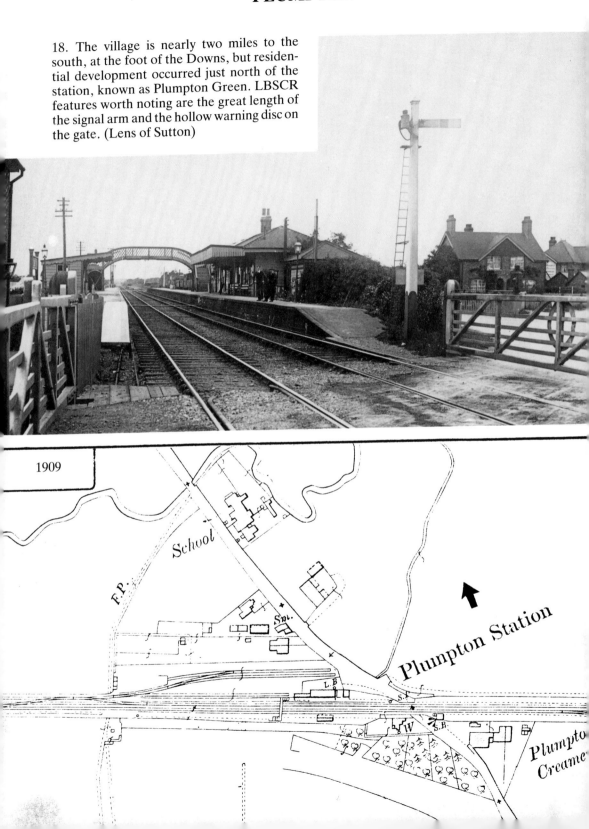

1909

School

F.P.

Plumpton Station

L B

W

Plumpto
Creame

19. Looking in the opposite direction, towards Lewes, we see a horse box at the cattle dock; a partly sheeted wagon on the goods shed road and class 12 4–4–2T no.19 heading an up express. The field on the right was the site of Plumpton racecourse – an important, if only a seasonal, source of railway revenue. (Lens of Sutton)

20. Those posing in this period photograph could have never dreamed that the entire station, footbridge and signal box would become "listed grade II buildings". The signal box is currently for sale whilst only a few trains now call in the rush hours (as at Cooksbridge). Numerous milk churns stand outside the creamery – a reminder of this once important railway traffic.
(Lens of Sutton)

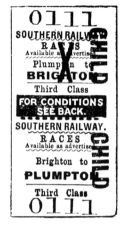

21. One of the massive 4–6–4 Baltic tanks, no. 2333, drifts in with an up train on 3rd March 1934. The postman, with cycle clips on, reminds us of the important part the stopping train once played in local mail distribution. About 1910, an additional footbridge and up platform was built a few yards to the west of the original, for use on race days. (H.C. Casserley)

COOKSBRIDGE

22. Agricultural traffic was of prime importance in this thinly populated district. The large dimensions of the goods shed and the lack of platform awning indicate the value of freight traffic in relation to passengers at this station. (Lens of Sutton)

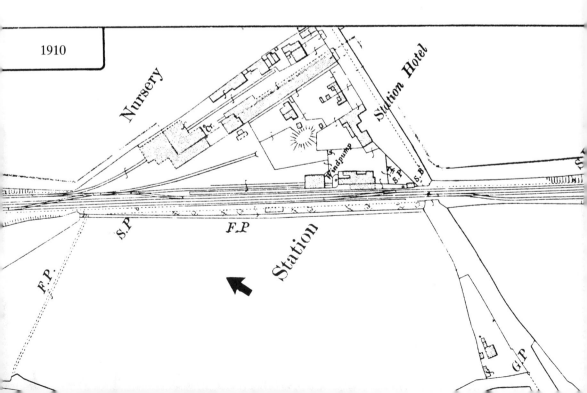

1910

Station, Cooksbridge.

23. As at Plumpton, the main station buildings are on the down side and remain intact today. By the time this post card was produced, passengers had the benefit of a platform canopy. (Lens of Sutton)

25. A 1975 view shows the A275 to be then protected by lifting barriers and the station to have been recently painted. When it became unstaffed, the signalman issued tickets but now the box has been closed. (J. Scrace)

24. No. 326 *Grosvenor* races past the typical round-ended LBSCR wagons, with a down boat train for Newhaven. The lamp post has mysteriously lost its lamp.
(E.J. Bedford/Bluebell Archives)

LEWES

26. The complicated history of three successive stations is explained with diagrams in our *Brighton to Eastbourne* album. Here we offer some photographs of the part of the station relating to the Haywards Heath line, not relevant to the previous album. We look east Swiss chalet style and is visible on the left. (E.J. Bedford/NRM)

27. The severe curvature of the track seen in this and the previous photograph was reduced when the third and present station was built in 1889. Ballast over the sleepers was eventually banned by the Railway Inspectorate as rotting timbers could remain undetected. (E.J. Bedford/NRM)

28. Crowds gather on 24th September 1879 to gaze at no.174, a 2–4–0 built in 1864 by Craven, after the explosion of its firebox, whilst hauling the 2.05pm Hastings to Victoria train. Subsequent inspection showed that the spring balance safety valves had been interfered with and this resulted in the death of the driver. He was blown onto the roof of the second vehicle – hence the ladder. (O.J. Morris/Lens of Sutton)

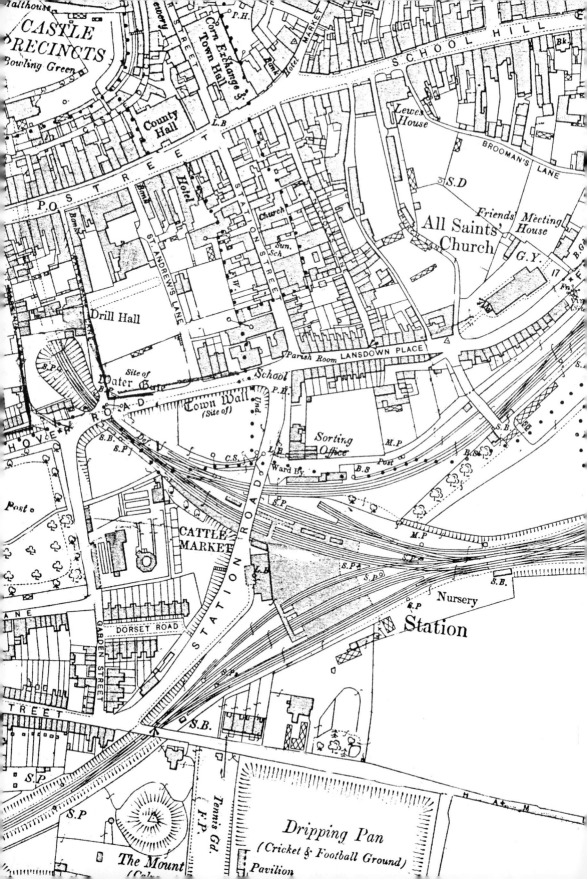

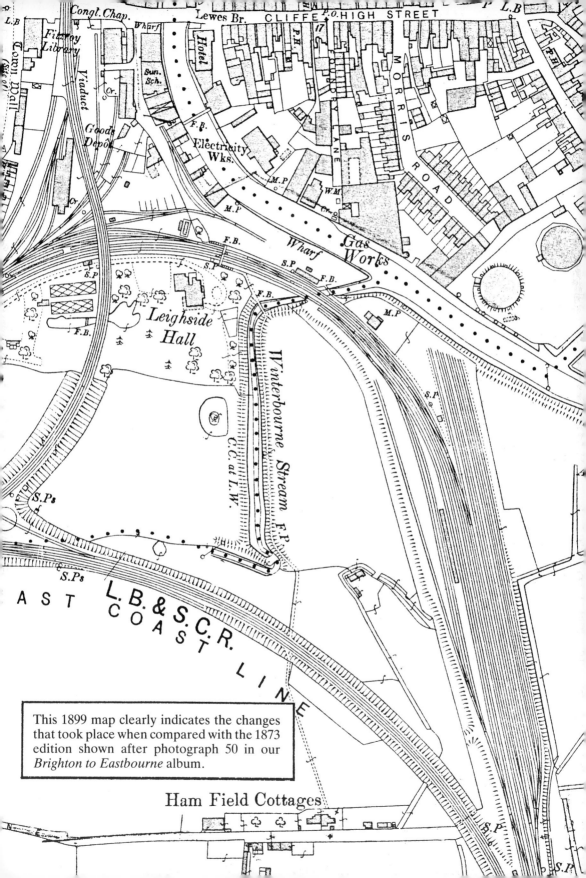

This 1899 map clearly indicates the changes that took place when compared with the 1873 edition shown after photograph 50 in our *Brighton to Eastbourne* album.

Ham Field Cottages

29. An historic event – the first train to enter the rebuilt station on 17th June 1889. It is the down newspaper train and is witnessed by onlookers on the road bridge. (E.J. Bedford/NRM)

30. The fine contrasting brickwork has become shabby and the carriage canopy has been lost but otherwise the handsome exterior remains little altered today. Whilst cabs await passengers, a child departs in a cycle trailer. (Lens of Sutton)

31. H.R.H. The Prince of Wales is about to return to London after a visit to Lewes Summer Races in 1897. An interesting detail is the buttoned plush upholstery on the door of the 1st class compartment. The LBSCR Royal Train was not built until the following year. (E.J. Bedford/NRM)

32. Looking east from Station Road bridge, we see the new down platform in the bottom right corner and the former down platform in the centre of the picture. The tracks were retained as a loop for goods trains. (O.J. Morris/Lens of Sutton)

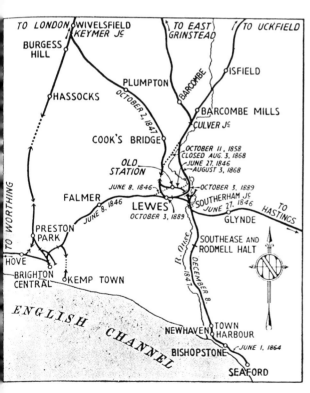

(Railway Magazine)

33. A class C3 0–6–0 heads on up freight on the goods loop whilst a class D1 0–4–2T is in the down loop with a push-pull train for Seaford on 2nd June 1923. A curious accident occurred at this point on 5th August 1950 when a class C2X no. 32441 was leaving the up goods loop and collided with the 9.16pm from Horsted Keynes to Seaford, of which the rear two coaches were unlit. The signalman had overlooked the fact that the train was composed of *three* 2NOL sets instead of the usual two! (Late E. Wallis)

35. Class 13 no. 2075 leaves with a Victoria to Eastbourne train, composed of LBSCR stock, on 22nd April 1935. Horse boxes in the background remind us of the proximity of Lewes Racecourse, a useful source of railway revenue. (S.W. Baker)

34. A 1929 view showing the extensive awning over the up platform and the palatial "Gents" on the down island platform. Don't be distracted from the splendid vaulted roof covering the central area of the station. (E.R. Lacey collection)

36. 37. These photographs, taken in 1935, show alterations in progress prior to electrification. The platforms were lengthened; the goods loop junction drastically altered; a new signal box built; Southover Road bridge reconstructed and the tunnel entrance widened. (British Rail) (H.F. Wheeller)

38. The castle in the background has witnessed many changes, not least on the railway scene. The unusual make up of this train is explained by the fact that it is a theatrical special – vans for the props and scenery with some coaches for the performers. When D6522 was photographed Eastbourne-bound on 11th October 1964, the era of such specials was nearly ended. (S.C. Nash)

39. Only the former Lewes Junction signal box survives and is now in use as a panel box. The 4HAP unit forms the 11.51 Seaford to Brighton service on 5th April 1983 and is about to enter the platform 7. In the foreground is the "up Brighton loop" to platform 8 and an electrified carriage siding. (J. Scrace)

41. Looking in the opposite direction, also in 1924, we see the cutting through an outcrop of chalk, beyond which is Southerham Junction. Students of signalling will note the long-forgotten Coligny-Welch distant indicators. (Late E. Wallis) ⟶

(In 1985, the platforms were renumbered 1 to 5.)

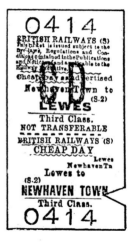

40. Lewes East Box had 33 levers and controlled the junction of the 11-road goods yard (in the distance) with the main line to the station (curving to the left). In 1937, there were 48 goods trains received each week and 38 were despatched. (Late E. Wallis)

42. North of the cutting, the line crossed the River Ouse on what was originally a timber drawbridge. In the background is the cement works, which sent much of its production by barge to Newhaven to be loaded into ships. The Gas Company in Lewes also had the right to demand that this bridge was opened daily, as their coal supply had once been waterborne. When the SR proposed to change from gas to electric lighting at Lewes station, it is reported that the Gas Co. retaliated by threatening to enforce their bridge rights. Thus the station was gas lit until after nationalisation. (R. Randall collection)

43. Class 71 electric locomotive no. E5003 heads the Newhaven boat train on 29th August 1959. Concrete encasement of the steel piers had been necessary after they had been damaged by a barge in 1935. In 1942 the bridge was decked to allow military vehicles to cross it in an emergency. (S.C. Nash)

44. Southerham Junction was originally near the north end of the chalk cutting, quadruple track being provided until the Eastbourne and Seaford lines diverged. In 1976 the junction was moved to the south end of the cut-ting at the same time as a new road bridge was built. Class C3 0–6–0 no. 306 with an up freight for Willow Walk passes the signal box in about 1908. (E.R. Lacey collection)

45. Schools class no. 905 *Tonbridge* waits at the junction, ready to return to its home shed at St. Leonards after working a special train down to Newhaven. (C.C.B. Herbert)

46. A down Newhaven boat train hauled by class H1 no. 2037 and an ex-SECR D1 4–4–0 takes precedence over an up Eastbourne electric train at the divergence of the lines. (C.C.B. Herbert)

0030
SOUTHERN RAILWAY.
SUMMER TICKET
Available Calendar Month.
Seaford to
LONDON BRIDGE or
VICTORIA
Via Lingfield or Plumpton
(Issued at Denmark Hill)
Third Class

FOR CONDITIONS
SEE BACK

SOUTHERN RAILWAY.
SUMMER TICKET
Available as advertised.
Lon.B.or Vic.
Seaford
London Bridge or
Victoria to
SEAFORD
Via Lingfield or Plumpton
(Issued at Denmark Hill)
Third Class
0030

BRITISH RAILWAYS (S)
This ticket is issued subject to the Bye-laws,
Regulations and Conditions contained in the
Publications and Notices of and applicable to the
Railway Executive.
Seaford to
LEWES
Third Class. Fare 11½d
NOT TRANSFERABLE

6184

6184

47. This Stroudley D1 was one of several fitted with Spencer's Patent Buffers designed to prevent buffer locking when working pull and push trains. On 11th December 1929, when propelling the 10.24 Lewes to Seaford, it collided with C2X 0–6–0 no. B546, a light engine crossing from the goods yard near Lewes East, causing injury to 12 passengers. (Dr. I.C. Allen)

1929 map 6″ to 1 mile.

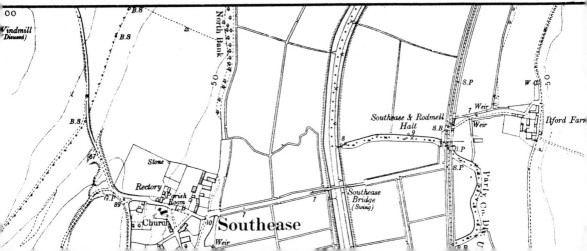

48. Opened as Southease & Rodmell Halt on 1st September 1906, it was served for a limited period by two petrol railcars built by Dick Kerr & Co. Normally push-pull trains called until the advent of electrification. Until 1960 the signal box was known as Itford Crossing, after a nearby farm. In 1973, multiple warning lights replaced the level crossing gates. (Lens of Sutton)

49. A 1984 northward view shows the Ouse Valley in the distance. The station ("halt" is out of fashion) is situated on an island, with the navigable Ouse to the west and a backwater to the east. Tiny Southease is more than ½ mile distant and Rodmell is a further ½ mile. (C. Wilson)

NEWHAVEN NORTH QUAY

50. As there are several interesting features to be studied before reaching Newhaven Town, we have included them in a separate section. Newhaven North Box later became 'A' Box and was on the west side of the line.

Class E4 no. 2508 hurries past with a down stopping train composed of three ex-SECR coaches and three ex-LSWR, on 7th August 1932. (H.F. Wheeller)

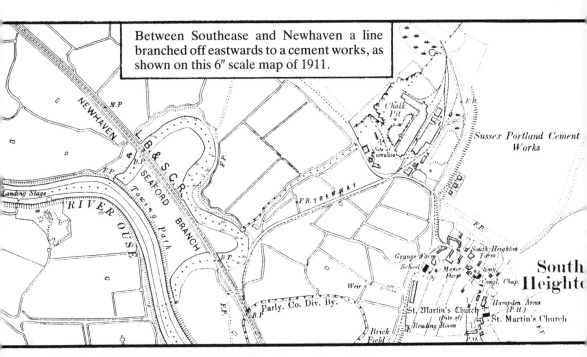

Between Southease and Newhaven a line branched off eastwards to a cement works, as shown on this 6″ scale map of 1911.

51. Seen from 'A' Box in 1950, class H2 no. 32421 *South Foreland* increases the momentum of th heavy up boat train. In the right background are Cedar Sidings, where many coaches were scrapped. The rail-served North Quay was opened in 1891 and was mainly used for timber traffic. (S.C. Nash)

52. This earlier photograph shows "Gladstone" 0–4–2 no. 190 *Arthur Otway* easing the 9.45am Grand Vitesse freight train for London (Willow Walk) out of the up yard on 7th July 1913. This was an overnight service from Paris, particularly used for perishable goods. (R.C. Riley collection)

53. An ex-LSWR 3rd brake and in the distance an ex-SECR van in departmental stock await the attentions of the scrapmen at Cedar Sidings in July 1950. As at Barry, much of the scrap steel departed by sea, notably to Spain. (S.C. Nash)

54. After working the final train on the West Quay branch on 10th August 1963, the ageing Terrier shunts condemned stock at Town Sidings. At the north end of the down sidings, there used to be a lightly laid line to Denton Cement Works, closed in 1914. Entry was through a normally locked gate and in World War I the area was used for ammunition storage. On one occasion *Fenchurch* became derailed and soldiers formed a human chain with buckets of water to avert the dangerous consequences of throwing the fire out. It took four hours to rerail, by which time it was dark and the gate had been locked. The second mishap of the day occurred – the locomotive smashed through the gate! (R.C. Riley)

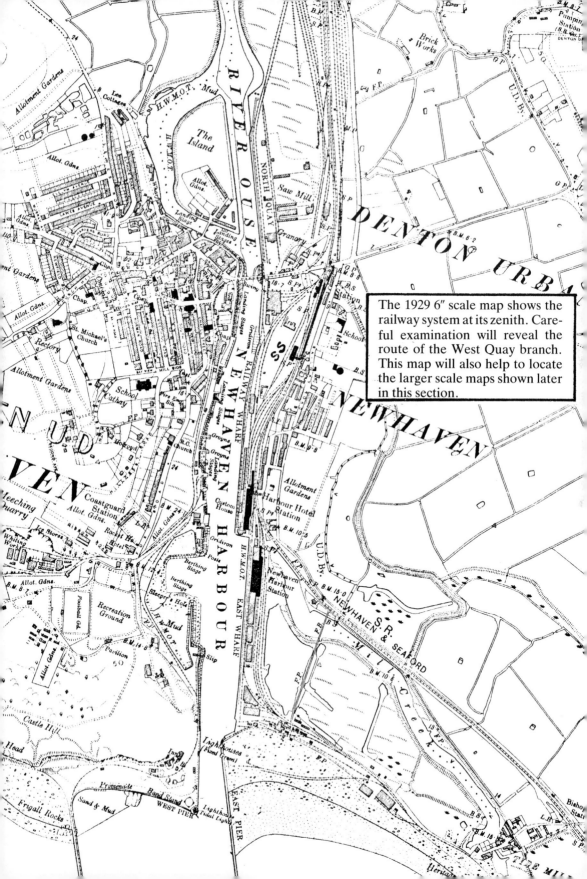

The 1929 6" scale map shows the railway system at its zenith. Careful examination will reveal the route of the West Quay branch. This map will also help to locate the larger scale maps shown later in this section.

55. A wooden drawbridge stood at this site from 1794 until replaced by this swing bridge in December 1866. By 1879 it carried the West Harbour railway in addition to the coast road. The latter was realigned onto a new high level bridge in 1976 and the swing bridge was demolished.
(R.C. Riley collection)

London Brighton & South Coast Railway.

Waldron to
Newhaven Harbour

56. *Fenchurch*, now bearing its later SR number, leaves the North Yard to take a trip along the A259 to the swing bridge. South Box is on the right. (C.C.B. Herbert)

57. On the north side of the line was the Railway Hotel. *Fenchurch* returns from the West Quay on 12th July 1950, bearing her lengthy BR number, whilst the shunter/flagman looks on. Until WWII he walked ahead of the train, ringing a bell. The practice was discontinued during the war because of its more sinister implications and was never reintroduced. (R.C. Riley)

58. The same locomotive, but bearing its earlier SR number B636, creeps along the main road between the Fire Station, on the left, and the swing bridge cabin, on the right. (Dr. I.C. Allen)

59. *Fenchurch* features in many of the photographs as it was allocated to Newhaven continuously from 1898 to 1955. Here she crosses the eastern span of the bridge on 12th July 1950. (R.C. Riley)

60. Almost five years later, we see a sister Terrier at almost the same position. The boards parallel to the running rails could be lifted to gain access to tbe bridge turning mechanism. (P. Hay)

61. A 1971 view shows lifting barriers at the level crossing in the distance and a gang of eight men toiling to turn the capstan that opened the bridge. Curiously their motion was in the opposite direction of the moving span. The gas main had to be shut off at each end of the bridge and disconnected prior to its opening. There was sufficient gas retained in the isolated pipe to continue to illuminate the red-glazed lamp which was a warning to shipping. (E. Wilmshurst)

62. A few minutes later, the span was nearly open and the traffic queue had brought the town to a standstill. The span was usually turned in 3 minutes although road traffic was halted for about 10 minutes before the vessel passed. (E. Wilmshurst)

1910 map showing the Earl of Sheffield's Tramway.

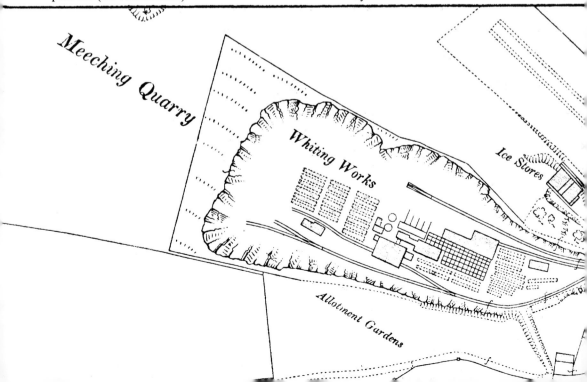

63. Around 1880, the Earl of Sheffield built a tramway to convey chalk from Meeching Quarry to the wharves. The map shows a whiting works and ice stores nearby. Ice for the latter came from Germany and consignments were known to come to Sussex from Scandinavia and even Newfoundland in the pre-refrigeration era. The track was standard gauge and entirely horse worked. In the background is the Sheffield Arms Hotel in Fort Road. (A.J. Parsons collection)

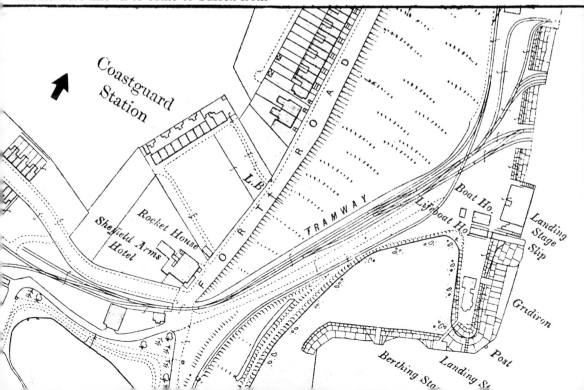

64. In addition to a tarpaulin and rope works, the branch served an oil depot established in 1928 to supply the first oil-fired ferry – the MV *Worthing*. The principal function of the branch was to convey materials for breakwater maintenance. (Lens of Sutton)

66. Sidings at the sea shore were used for loading ballast, hence the two early LBSCR ballast wagons ahead of *Fenchurch*. The canvas flaps over their axle boxes protected the bearings from the effects of stone dust. Could the lady have been the driver's wife and if so had she traversed the line on the cramped footplate in her Sunday best? (Lens of Sutton)

←————————

65. Looking north from Castle Hill, we see, on the left, a lagoon known as Sleeper's Hole; in the foreground, the West Quay branch on its way to the breakwater (earlier it took a direct route across the mouth of Sleeper's Hole); in the centre is the tall London & Paris Hotel and on the right is the East Quay of 1886. (R.C. Riley collection)

0 2 1 7
SOUTHERN RAILWAY.
Commercial Traveller
Available on Day of issue only,
Newhaven Harbour or
Town to
BRIGHTON
Third Class
FOR CONDITIONS
SEE BACK
SOUTHERN RAILWAY.
Day Commercial
Traveller.
Available on Day of issue only
Brighton to
NEWHAVEN
HARBOUR or TOWN
Third Class
0 2 1 7

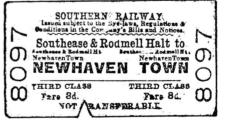

SOUTHERN RAILWAY.
Issued subject to the Bye-laws, Regulations &
Conditions in the Company's Bills and Notices.
Southease & Rodmell Halt to
8097
Southease & Rodmell Ht.
Newhaven Town
Southease & Rodmell Ht.
Newhaven Town
NEWHAVEN TOWN
8097
THIRD CLASS
Fare 8d.
THIRD CLASS
Fare 8d.
NOT TRANSFERABLE

67. Rounding the headland at the foot of the cliffs, the line passed a store for building materials before reaching the massive breakwater. This could be an aggressive and turbulent location in mid-winter. (C.C.B. Herbert)

68. The 2800ft. long breakwater was completed in 1889 after many years of construction work. It coincided with the introduction of a non tide-dependent shipping timetable in time for the expected increase in traffic for the Paris Exhibition. (R.C. Riley collection)

69. The slotted post signal with Saxby &
Farmer lamp was provided to control shipping. The post and lighthouse are visible in
the previous photograph.
(E.R. Lacey collection)

70. Last day of the Newhaven West Quay branch when no. 32678 cleared all remaining wagons from the line, 10th August 1963. From left to right, a harbour employee, the fireman, Driver Maurice Smith and shunter/flagman. Demolition commenced almost at once but wagons used the engineers' yard just across the swing bridge for a time, being conveyed to and from it by a steam crane as no light locomotives remained at Newhaven. The driver on the branch was usually the senior driver at the depot.
(R.C. Riley collection)

71. Happier days on the breakwater line with Craven A cigarettes advertised on the kiosk and no doubt cups of tea and ice cream available. The unusual numerals came from an unused supply of LBSCR gilt numerals unearthed at Brighton Works and applied to several small engines in 1935, even to some of LSWR origin. (C.C.B. Herbert)

72. By the date of this photograph, 5th May 1960, the 'Terriers' were supplied by Brighton shed changing about once a fort-night for boiler washout purposes. On this occasion 32635, formerly DS377, the former Brighton Works pilot in the splendour of Stroudley livery was in charge of this train propelled on to the breakwater, one sus-pects, for photographic purposes by the late Maurice Smith. By 1963 the breakwater track was unfit for use. (W.M.J. Jackson)

NEWHAVEN TOWN

73. A placid horse waits untroubled by the resident iron house shunting a ballast brake van and no doubt a rake of clattering wagons. The gates were replaced by lifting barriers in December 1964. (R.C. Riley collection)

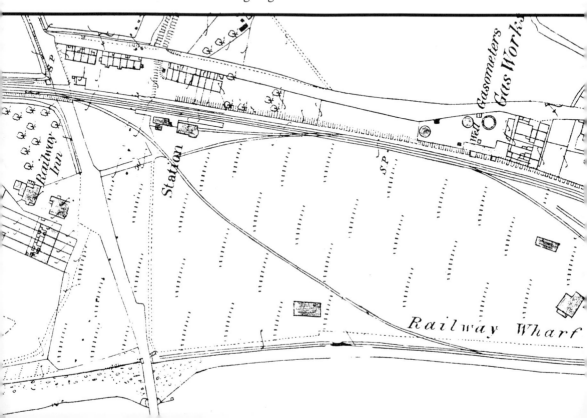

74. Looking north from station footbridge in about 1911, we gain a glimpse of the sizeable goods shed for local traffic and witness the departure of a train for Lewes, propelled by A1 class 0–6–0T no. 674. To the left of the "Balloon" coach is the West Quay line curving away behind the hedge.
(R.C. Riley collection)

This undated map shows Mill Creek on the extreme right. This was filled in when East Quay was constructed and a step was formed in the line of the water frontage. This remains today and has been put to good use for the end loading of ferries. The route of the proposed branch to Seaford has been superimposed on this copy.

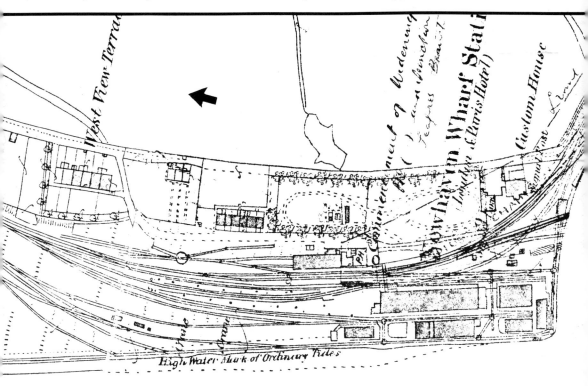

75. Viewed from the same point on 18th August 1911, class C2X no. 550 takes the curve leading to the locomotive shed having worked a freight train from Willow Walk. The background contains some period rolling stock and the hills of the eastern flank of the Ouse Gap. (R.C. Riley collection)

77. Class E4 no. 2503 arrives from Brighton with an unusual train composed of an ex-LSWR van, two loaded open carriage trucks, a SR coach and an ex-LSWR coach. As no. 32503 this engine remained at Newhaven well into BR days. The up starting signals and crossing illumination methods are worth comparing with earlier photographs. (Dr. I.C. Allen) ⟶

76. From the footbridge steps one can appreciate the bulk of "Baltic" tank no. 2332 as she runs through, buffers gleaming, with a down Sunday boat train, on 14th April 1933. (S.W. Baker)

78. The wide chimney on this Schools class *Harrow* was for the Lemaitre blastpipe. These locomotives would just fit onto the Newhaven turntable, whereas the King Arthur class had to run to Brighton to turn. The train is empty stock for a special up boat train on 25th April 1954. (S.C. Nash)

79. Today the station retains its old buildings on the up side (on the right) and some semaphore signals, but the down platform has only a glass "bus shelter". (Lens of Sutton)

80. An ex-LBSCR class D3 0-4-4T with ex-SECR coaches made an unusual sight on 12th November 1950, reviving memories of push and pull working 15 years earlier. Their presence was due to Sunday engineering work which necessitated loss of current. (S.C. Nash)

81. The locomotive shed was opened in 1887 and is seen here in 1908 to house E1 0–6–0T no. 123 and C2 0–6–0 no. 554, the latter being rebuilt to class C2X in 1911. We seem to have encountered the lady on the left before, on the West Quay branch.
(Lens of Sutton)

L B S C Ry.
Available on the Date of Issue ONLY
SEE CONDITIONS AT BACK
NEWHAVEN HARBOUR
TO
NEWHAVEN TOWN n.t.
1d. THIRD CLASS. 1d.
7745   7745

82. *Arthur Otway*, one of the Gladstone class, is seen being prepared on 16th April 1911. On the skyline are the massive sheer legs which were often used for lifting components of the Cross Channel ferries as well as the Isle of Wight ferries from Portsmouth. Prior to 1901, some of the ship repair work was undertaken in Brighton Locomotive Works. (R.C. Riley collection)

83. *Fenchurch*, in its latter day Newhaven Harbour Co. livery of black with red lining, stands outside the shed, with the Marine Workshops in the background. Until 1919, the Harbour Co. engines were housed in a separate shed on the East Quay.
(Lens of Sutton)

84. The 60ft. turntable was installed in 1917 to accommodate the K class, then used on the Willow Walk freights. No. 337 was the first to be built (in 1913) and was in use until 1962. Behind the engine is a Jablachkoff candle, an arc light of the type that would have earlier hung from the pole seen in photograph no.77.
(British Rail)

85. An ex-LBSCR K class stands over a pit on 19th April 1958. The emptiness of the shed is due to the fact that it was reduced to the status of a sub shed to Brighton in September 1955 after which only one BR 2–6–4T, two E4 0–6–2Ts and one A1X 0–6–0T were stabled there overnight. Note the brazier by the water column to prevent it freezing in winter. (R.C. Riley)

86. Amid the smoke of exploding detonators and suitably decorated after 65 years of service, the last Terrier leaves the shed on 18th August 1963. The shed closed completely on 9th September 1963 and was later used for commercial purposes. (R.C. Riley)

NEWHAVEN HARBOUR

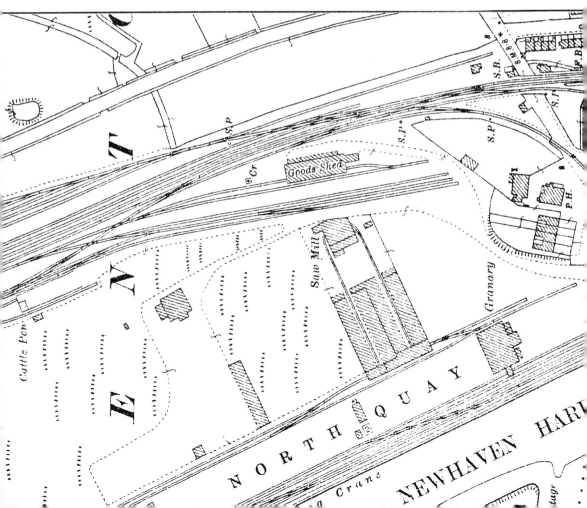

87. Class D1 0–4–2T no.2247 heads a Lewes-Seaford train on 11th October 1933. The station nameboard acknowledges the proximity of the London & Paris Hotel shown on the maps. It was opened in 1848 and in 1939 was requisitioned by the Navy. It was damaged during the War and demolished in 1956. The tower in the background supplied hydraulic power to the dockside cranes. (H.C. Casserley)

Marine dredged ballast is landed at North Quay and some is conveyed by rail to Crawley or Wimbledon in RMC bogie aggregate wagons.

1928 map continued overleaf →

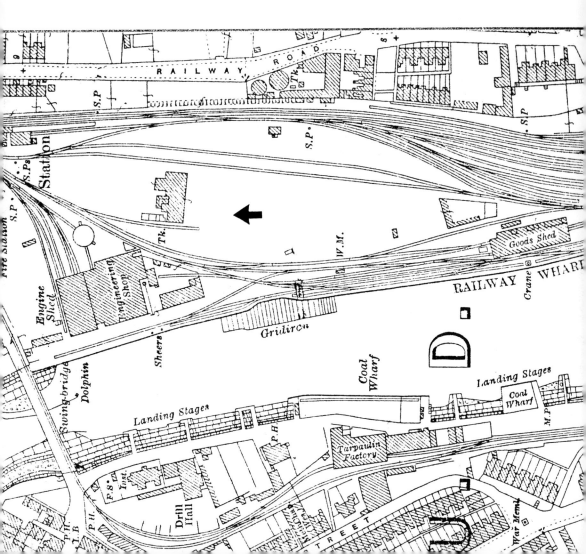

1928 map continued from previous page.

88. Another northward view shows a sign in English and French inviting passengers to alight for the Cross Channel Steamers. (Lens of Sutton)

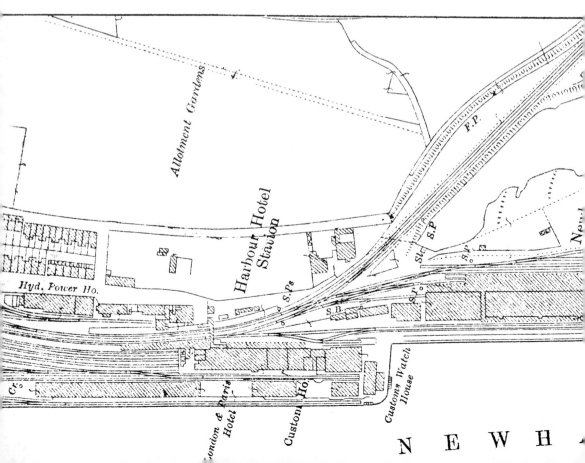

89. Looking south, we see the non-electrified siding to the East quay featured in the foreground of the previous view. The banner repeater signals on the footbridge relate to the signals seen in the next picture. (Lens of Sutton)

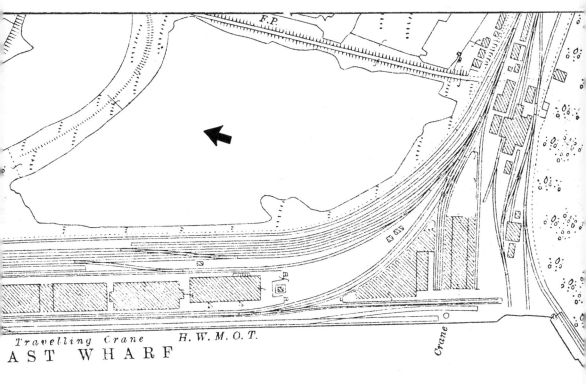

Travelling Crane *H. W. M. O. T.*

A S T   W H A R F

E N   H A R B O U R

90. Looking south from the footbridge, the Seaford line is seen diverging to the left; the terminus for the boat trains is to the left of the signal box and the London & Paris Hotel is on the extreme right. (J.J. Smith)

91. This is the LBSCR Marsh elliptical-roofed boat train set no. 87, complete with roof destination boards. This set was built in 1907 and had some distinctive features. It included two 2nd Class brakes, a 3rd Class brake and the unique full brake no. 191 nearest to the camera. The prevalence of brakes was due to there being a portion for London Bridge in pre-1914 years, and also vast quantities of luggage to convey. The boat trains retained 1st, 2nd and 3rd Class into BR days. (National Railway Museum)

London Brighton & South Coast Railway.

Dormans to

Newhaven Town

92. A smartly turned out class I4 waits to leave with an up boat train. This photograph was probably taken soon after no.33 was built in 1908, as these locomotives were remarkably unsuccessful and were soon transferred to lesser duties. (Lens of Sutton)

93. The area south of the London & Paris Hotel was reclaimed in the 1880s from marshland, including the Tides Mill Creek. East Quay and this fine terminal station were built theron. No. 193 *Freemantle* waits with empty stock which includes an American Pullman Car. These cars were first used on the LBSCR in 1881, many surviving today as holiday homes on the South Coast. (E.R. Lacey collection)

94. Terrier no.2647 stands beside the Customs Sheds. Note the diminutive shunting box on the left, in effect a covered ground frame. No. 2647 spent most of its life in SR days at Newhaven. In BR days it was realised what a low mileage the Newhaven Terriers worked and in April 1951 no. 2647 was sent to Fratton for the Hayling Island line on which it broke a crank axle, with disastrous results as no steam crane was allowed on the branch. It was withdrawn in October 1951.
(C.C.B. Herbert)

→

96. Although the Seaford line was electrified in 1935 the line to the Marine Station continued to be steam worked because of the lack of flexibility in the fixed unit EMU formations. After the war electric locomotives were available, Ashford 1941-built CC1/2 (later BR nos. 20001/2), joined in 1948 by no. 20003. The third rail was extended to the Marine Station in 1949 and on 14th May 'Schools' class 4–4–0 no. 30929 *Malvern* hauled the last scheduled steam boat train. No. 20003 inaugurated the new service the following day, although the relief boat trains remained steam worked for several years. No. 20002 has just arrived with the down morning train from Victoria, 28th May 1949. The Newhaven men always referred to these engines as "Hornbys". (S.W. Baker)

95. Class H2 4-4-2 no. 2422 *North Foreland* at the head of an up boat train at the Marine Station in the mid 1930s, with the Customs Shed in the background. These 1911 Brighton Atlantics were still working relief boat trains 20 years later. (C.C.B. Herbert)

97. Later, from 1959, the class 71 locomotives helped out, joined in 1962 by the class 73 electro-diesels. Class 73 no. E6042 (later 73114) stands at the later platform by the Customs Sheds having worked the 9.50am from Victoria, on 28th September 1969. By this time the East Quay had been dramatically changed by the road vehicle roll-on roll-off facilities. Since 4th October 1970 the boat train has been EMU worked. (J. Scrace)

98. The current appearance of the Marine Station. New buildings have been erected and the old Customs Shed demolished, a new one being located near the site of the former Hotel, 5th April 1983. The level crossing nearby was resited in 1978. (J. Scrace)

RAILWAY SHIPPING

99. The French Ouest Railway was a partner with the LBSCR in the ferry service and so it would appear that it was cheaper to have their new locomotive brought by rail from the builders, Neilson & Co, in Glasgow than to have it shipped directly from that city, as was normally done with Neilson's orders. Staff pose proudly under the Marine Workshop's sheer legs, in 1883.
(National Railway Museum)

100. The P.S. *Brittany* of 1882. Note the tall rail-mounted crane, the London and Paris Hotel in the background and the prevalence of square-rigged vessels on the west bank. This was a sister ship of the *Normandy* and these vessels were the first to be fitted with Stroudley's greatly improved feathering paddle wheel. Both were sold in 1902.
(R.C. Riley collection)

101. The P.S. *Brighton* built in Govan in 1878, moored on the west bank. She was a sister ship of the P.S. *Victoria* which ran aground near the French coast in 1887 and gradually broke up. The P.S. *Brighton* was sold after an accident in Dieppe Harbour in 1893 but was repaired and carried out mine-laying duties in WWI. On the East Quay we see P.S. *Paris* and P.S. *Rouen*, both built in 1888, the last paddle steamers on this route. (R.C. Riley collection)

102. The T.S. *Brighton* of 1903, built by Denny of Dumbarton, leaving the harbour about 1910. This was the first turbine ship on the route to Dieppe but had been preceded by a few months by the SECR's first turbine ship *The Queen* on the Dover-Calais route. T.S. *Brighton* remained in service until 1930. (R.C. Riley collection)

103. T.S. *Dieppe*, slightly larger, entered traffic two years later and was photographed on 2nd January 1911. The LBSCR had secured a Royal Mail contract in 1898 and remarkably as early as 1906 140 motor cars were carried by the ships on this route. This shows a good view of the Marine Workshops, and the sheer legs. T.S. *Dieppe* survived until 1935.

104. The T.S. *Versailles* of 1919 leaves for Dieppe, 14th April 1935, giving a better view of the rail-mounted crane on the East Quay. The French-owned ship was involved in the Dunkirk evacuation but was damaged by bombs and had to go to Brest for repair. Later it went to Nantes whence it was towed to Germany. In September 1945 a Dieppe crew was sent to Flensburg to recover her but she was found to have two metres of water in her and was considered to be beyond economic repair. (S.W. Baker)

NEWHAVEN EAST QUAY

105. No. 2636 makes a rare visit to the East Quay line from Newhaven Town in 1937. During WWI *Fenchurch* was used to haul ambulance trains from the East Quay to the Town station. (C.C.B. Herbert)

←

106. Remarkably this sign was erected near Tide Mills Reach in 1956, a year after No. 32636, the former *Fenchurch*, had left the district. The East Quay line was still restricted to the A1X class but traffic was negligible consisting only of the occasional ballast wagon. (A.R. Grierson)

→

The 1910 map shows the Tide Mills branch running through village street and another line parallel to the shore. The latter was used mainly for collecting shingle and was an extension of the East Quay line.

BISHOPSTONE BEACH

107. This station was built for the residents of Tide Mills village. A siding ran to Bishopstone Tide Mills which was worked by the Newhaven Harbour Co. engine. The Tide Mills ceased grinding in 1883, the store houses remaining in use until 1900, after which the siding was progressively lifted. In August 1922 the station was renamed Bishopstone Halt and in 1938 Bishopstone Beach Halt. There was formerly a signal box at the Seaford end of the down platform controlling the level crossing and sidings, which were lifted about 1922. Tide Mills village was evacuated in 1940 when the Royal Navy took over the harbour. The Halt was closed from 1st January 1942 and this view looking towards Seaford was taken in July 1947, since when it has been demolished. (R.W. Kidner)

108. An E4 0–6–2T ambles across the former marshland on its way back from Seaford on 26th September 1953. Goods services to Seaford ceased on 4th May 1964. (J.J. Smith)

109. Another photograph to portray the treeless windswept environment. The massive shingle banks were a source of ballast for construction purposes but are small when compared with the Crumbles or Dungeness. Eight coaches with a buffet is not the normal make up for the basic hourly service. (C. Wilson)

BISHOPSTONE

110. Built ½ mile to the east of the previous station, the new SR style of architecture is evident on the ground floor but the apparent provision of gun slits in the tower is unexpected. The station was opened on 26th September 1938 but the anticipated residential development was delayed by WWII and post war shortages. An up pull and push train with D1 class no.2244 propelling ex-LBSCR motor set no.758 was machine-gunned near here on 3rd July 1940. The train was little damaged by the driver was fatally injured. (Lens of Sutton)

BRITISH RAILWAYS
-BISHOPSTONE-

111. An enthusiasts special enters the first cutting on the branch en route for Seaford on 7th October 1962. This special saw the welcome – if temporary – return of *Fenchurch*. It is seen piloting class E6 0–6–2T no.32418 which, despite its immaculate appearance, was only in service for another two months. (S.C. Nash)

112. *Fenchurch*, yet again, leaves Seaford in April 1931 hauling a lengthy freight near the summit of the 1 in 100 descent to Bishopstone. (Dr. I.C. Allen)

113. *Seaford* stands at Seaford in 1874 a few months before its withdrawal. Built in 1846 by Bodmer, it received its name when rebuilt by Stroudley in 1871. The gong on the tender was part of the Stroudley - Rusbridge patented communication system, in use before the advent of continous brakes.
(R.C. Riley collection)

1899

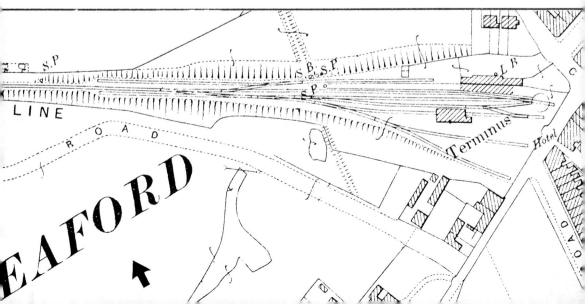

114. The well proportioned buildings remain basically unaltered today and is still the signing on point for six train crews. This Edwardian postcard reminds us of a more leisurely era. (M.G. Joly collection)

115. Terrier no. 84 *Crowborough* turns into the small goods yard on the south side of the terminus before the line was doubled and an additional yard provided on the north side. The signal is in a slotted post with the separate Saxby & Farmer gas lamp at lower level. (R.C. Riley collection)

116. A typical LBSCR terminal scene with a class D3 gently simmering in the summer sun. The first goods shed, visible on the right, was due to be demolished in 1986 to make way for a new Health Centre.
(R.C. Riley collection)

117. A last look at *Fenchurch* in this album. Here she shunts an ex-SECR Birdcage set in April 1931, with her lamps reversed on her tall lamp irons. She can now be seen working on the Bluebell Railway, sometimes hauling similar coaches. (Dr. I.C. Allen)

118. Class C2 no. 2439 arrives with three former LSWR coaches on 14th August 1934. At the end of the line there was a sector plate, shown as a turntable on the maps. This ceased to be needed with the advent of electrification. (H.F. Wheeller)

1927

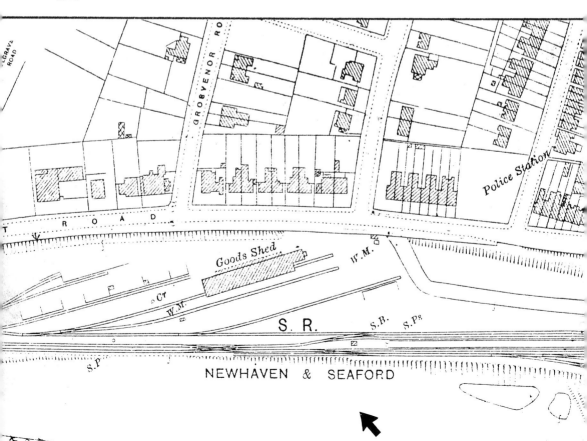

119. Terrier no. 32678, complete with a spark arrester of the type used to prevent Hayling bridge igniting, accelerates away with two vans of school luggage – another long forgotten source of railway revenue – on 25th July 1963. This is thought to have been the last steam train at this quiet Sussex resort. (S.C. Nash)

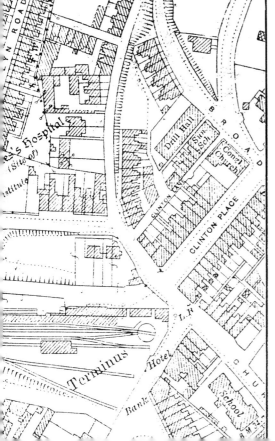

120. Two electrified sidings remain in use for carriage stabling – one visible on the right and one at the bay on the left. The previous photographs show the canopy to have been lengthened and then shortened again but fortunately, unlike many branch lines, a train service still operates. (J. Scrace)

MP MIDDLETON PRESS

EVOLVING THE ULTIMATE RAIL ENCYCLOPEDIA

Easebourne Lane, Midhurst, West Sussex.
GU29 9AZ   Tel:01730 813169

www.middletonpress.co.uk   email:info@middletonpress.co.uk

A-0 906520   B-1 873793   C-1 901706   D-1 904474

OOP Out of Print at time of printing - Please check current availability   **BROCHURE AVAILABLE SHOWING NEW TITLES**